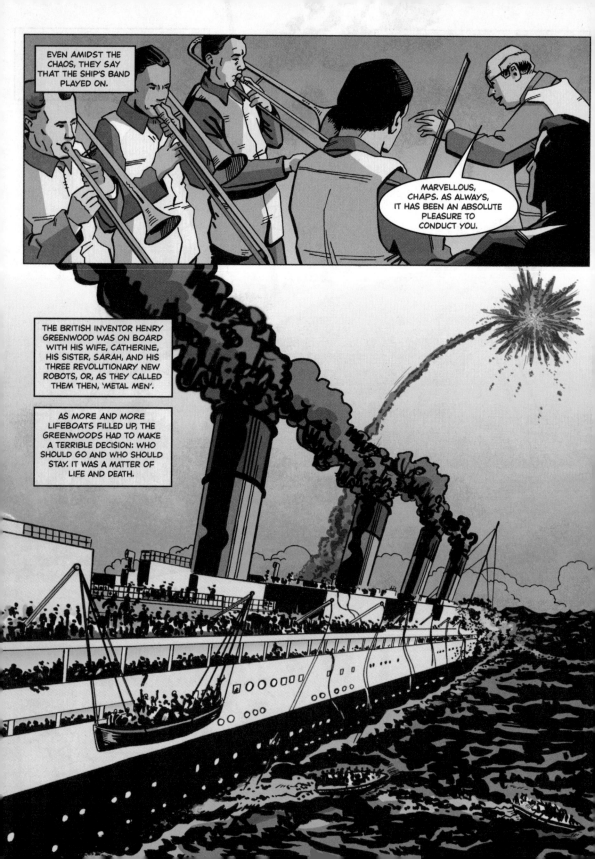

THE *COLOSSUS* CAME TO REST ON THE SEABED UNDER 4,000 METRES OF WATER. AT LEAST 1,500 LIVES WERE LOST IN THE DISASTER, AND EVEN MORE WOULD HAVE PERISHED IF IT WERE NOT FOR THE METAL MEN.

BUT NOBODY KNOWS WHAT HAPPENED TO OUR ROBOT HEROES...

EXCEPT FOR METAL MAN NUMBER TWO. HE SURVIVED THE SHIPWRECK.

AT SOME POINT HE MUST HAVE FOUND TWO OF HENRY GREENWOOD'S WATERTIGHT SUITCASES AND SET OFF TO FINISH HIS JOURNEY ON FOOT.

ALTHOUGH METAL MAN NUMBER TWO WAS LARGELY UNDAMAGED, HIS INTERNAL COMPASS WAS BROKEN, SO HE DIDN'T KNOW WHERE HE WAS HEADING.

FOR SIXTY YEARS HE TRAVELLED ACROSS THE OCEAN FLOOR LOOKING FOR THE PORT OF NEW NORTHWICH, HIS ORIGINAL DESTINATION, WHICH WE KNOW NOW AS ROBOT CITY.

HIS INTERNAL JOURNEY LOG SUGGESTS THAT HE ENCOUNTERED MANY CHALLENGING SITUATIONS.

HE WOULD HAVE SEEN SHIPS PASS OVERHEAD MANY TIMES, BUT HE WOULD HAVE BEEN UNABLE TO CONTACT THEM.

HE MAY HAVE HAD CLOSE CONTACT WITH MANY STRANGE SEA CREATURES.

BUT HE KEPT GOING.

NOTHING COULD STOP HIM.

AND THAT'S WHY METAL MAN NUMBER TWO IS KNOWN AS *GREENWOOD'S INDESTRUCTIBLE METAL MAN!*

AND NOW, A CENTURY AFTER THE *COLOSSUS* WENT DOWN, WE CAN ALL SEE THE METAL MAN HERE IN ROBOT CITY. ..

FOR SIXTY YEARS, HE HAD COUNTED EVERY STEP OF HIS JOURNEY. IT WAS ALL RECORDED IN HIS INTERNAL LOG.

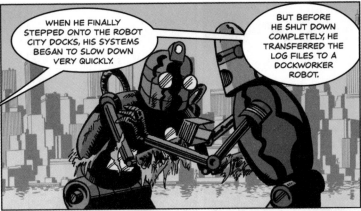

WHEN HE FINALLY STEPPED ONTO THE ROBOT CITY DOCKS, HIS SYSTEMS BEGAN TO SLOW DOWN VERY QUICKLY.

BUT BEFORE HE SHUT DOWN COMPLETELY, HE TRANSFERRED THE LOG FILES TO A DOCKWORKER ROBOT.

DR CROSS, DIDN'T ANY OTHER ROBOTS SURVIVE THE WRECK?

ARE YOU A PEOPLE DOCTOR OR A ROBOT DOCTOR?

HA, HA! I'M A DOCTOR OF ROBOT RESEARCH. I HAVE A PHD IN ROBOTICS.

NOW, THERE IS SOME EVIDENCE THAT SUGGESTS GREENWOOD'S TWO OTHER METAL MEN MAY HAVE SURVIVED. WHEN THE WRECK WAS LOCATED, THEY FOUND AN ARM FROM A METAL MAN, BUT NO BODY.

SO, WHERE ARE THEY NOW? ARE THEY IN ANOTHER MUSEUM?

THEY'VE NEVER BEEN FOUND, BUT EACH YEAR SAILORS REPORT SIGHTINGS OF THEM. ONE FISHERMAN IN NEW ZEALAND EVEN SAID HE'D SEEN ONE SWIMMING WITH DOLPHINS!

IT SEEMS UNLIKELY THAT THEY SURVIVED, THOUGH. THE CHANCES ARE THEY WERE BOTH DESTROYED WHEN THE SHIP SANK.

WELL, KIDS, THAT'S ABOUT IT FOR TODAY. I'M SORRY YOU CAN'T TOUCH THE INDESTRUCTIBLE MAN ANY MORE, BUT OUR SECURITY HAS TIGHTENED UP. DID YOU HEAR THAT ANNIE, THE ORIGINAL AUTOMETTE, WAS STOLEN LAST WEEK FROM ROBOT CITY MUSIC HALL? SO WE'RE BEING EXTRA-CAUTIOUS.

OUR INDESTRUCTIBLE MAN ISN'T GOING ANYWHERE, THANKS TO THIS NEW SECURITY GLASS.

MR FURNISS, SIR. I CAN CONFIRM THAT WE ARE IN POSSESSION OF ONE OF GREENWOOD'S METAL MEN.

EXCELLENT NEWS, MR GIFFORD. WHICH IS IT? ONE OR THREE?

IT'S GOT A CHIMNEY FUNNEL ON EACH SIDE OF ITS HEAD. DOES THAT MEAN IT'S NUMBER THREE?

IT DOES INDEED. WHAT CONDITION IS IT IN?

IT'S NOT OPERATIONAL. IT LOOKS LIKE IT HASN'T MOVED IN A WHILE, BUT IT'S ALL IN ONE PIECE AND THERE DOESN'T APPEAR TO BE ANY RUST.

THIS IS GOOD NEWS INDEED, MR GIFFORD. IT SOUNDS AS IF YOU'VE FOUND EXACTLY WHAT I NEED.

THANK YOU, MR FURNISS. WE ARE SETTING A COURSE FOR ROBOT CITY RIGHT NOW.

USE PIER 54, AS USUAL.

AND MAKE SURE YOU BRING HIM IN AT NIGHT. I DON'T WANT ANY JOURNALISTS SNIFFING AROUND.

I'VE BEEN WAITING FOR THIS MOMENT FOR YEARS. I WON'T LET A PRIZE LIKE THIS SLIP THROUGH MY FINGERS BECAUSE SOME SELF-RIGHTEOUS BUSYBODY COMES POKING HIS NOSE IN.

AT LAST, MY PLANS ARE ABOUT TO BE REALISED.

SIR, DO YOU THINK THE CUSTOMS OFFICERS WILL ASK QUESTIONS?

YOU WON'T HAVE ANY TROUBLE WITH THEM IF YOU BRING THE CARGO IN ON WEDNESDAY NIGHT.

WE HAVE AN ARRANGEMENT.

2:55 A.M., TWO NIGHTS LATER. ROBOT CITY.

THIS THING WEIGHS A TON! HOW ARE WE GOING TO MOVE IT?

WE MIGHT BE ABLE TO RESTORE SOME BASIC MOTOR FUNCTIONS IF WE CHARGE HIM UP.

GOOD IDEA. IT WOULD REALLY HELP US OUT IF HE COULD WALK A BIT.

LET'S SEE... I CAN ATTACH THE CABLE HERE.

HMMN. HARD TO READ THESE OLD SYSTEMS. I DON'T KNOW WHETHER HE'LL CHARGE LIKE A MODERN ROBOT.

WHO KNOWS, EH? LET'S TRY IT. OKAY--'CHARGE'.

ZZZSAAZ

MEANWHILE, AT THE ROBOTA MUSEUM OF ROBOT DEVELOPMENT.

OF COURSE, THIS MAY JUST BE A HOAX, BUT IF THERE REALLY IS ANOTHER INDESTRUCTIBLE OUT THERE WE'VE GOT TO FIND IT.

TRACE THAT SIGNAL, SARAH!

I'M PINPOINTING THE AREA IT'S BEING SENT FROM.

GOOD GRIEF. IT'S COMING FROM WITHIN ROBOT CITY!

THE VINEYARDS DISTRICT.

THERE WE GO. FINDING THE PRECISE LOCATION NOW. IT'S COMING FROM THE ESTATE OF...

TERENCE FURNISS! NOW, WHAT'S HE UP TO?

WE'VE GOT TO GET OVER THERE RIGHT AWAY WITH THE POLICE, THE NATIONAL GUARD, THE COASTGUARD... ANYBODY WHO CAN HELP.

WAIT JUST A MOMENT, DR CROSS. WE'RE NOT RUSHING OFF ANYWHERE.

WE HAVE SOME THINGS TO CONSIDER FIRST.

NOW, TERENCE FURNISS IS NOT A MAN TO BE CROSSED LIGHTLY.

YOU DO KNOW HE'S A MAJOR DONOR TO THE MUSEUM, DON'T YOU?

WE CAN'T AFFORD TO UPSET A MAN LIKE HIM.

IF WE GO CHARGING ONTO HIS PROPERTY, FURNISS IS NOT GOING TO APPRECIATE IT.

ON NO ACCOUNT ARE YOU TO CALL IN THE POLICE WITHOUT MY PERMISSION.

BUT SIR, IF FURNISS HAS MANAGED TO GET HOLD OF ANOTHER METAL MAN, THIS COULD BE CRUCIAL!

AGREED, TONY. BUT WE MUST TREAD CAREFULLY. I'M GOING TO MAKE SOME CALLS, AND I BELIEVE YOU'VE GOT A FEW OLD FRIENDS WHO MAY BE ABLE TO HELP, SARAH?

WE CAN'T JUST DO NOTHING, SIR.

I KNOW JUST WHO YOU MEAN.

THE WESTERN SEABOARD.

HELLO, ROBOT CITY CONFIDENTIAL INVESTIGATIONS. MIKE STONE SPEAKING.

MIKE! WE'RE NOT WORKING TODAY. I'M GETTING MARRIED IN AN HOUR!

SORRY, ROD. FORCE OF HABIT. THIS IS MIKE STONE, BEST MAN TO THE STARS, AT YOUR SERVICE!

MIKE, IT'S SARAH CROSS.

SARAH! HOW HAVE YOU BEEN? WE HAVEN'T SEEN YOU IN AGES.

MIKE, I NEED YOUR HELP WITH SOMETHING.

THAT MIGHT BE A PROBLEM, SARAH. WE'RE IN SAN VALENTINO RIGHT NOW FOR ROD'S WEDDING. BUT WHAT'S YOUR TROUBLE? PERHAPS WE CAN DO SOMETHING.

WHAT DO YOU KNOW ABOUT TERENCE FURNISS?

NOT A MAN TO GET TANGLED UP WITH, BY ALL ACCOUNTS. WE RECENTLY INVESTIGATED SOME KIDNAPPINGS OF HIGH-PROFILE ROBOTS, AND HIS NAME CROPPED UP ONCE OR TWICE. BE CAREFUL THERE.

HEY, SARAH. IT'S ROD. WE'RE HAVING A BIG PARTY WHEN WE GET BACK AFTER THE HONEYMOON. YOU SHOULD COME!

I'LL BE THERE. HAVE A WONDERFUL DAY, ROD. SEND MY LOVE TO ROSIE.

RIGHT. LOOKS LIKE IT'S DOWN TO ME. IF JAMES DOESN'T WANT ME TO CALL THE POLICE I'LL HAVE TO TAKE MATTERS INTO MY OWN HANDS.

LET'S SEE... TORCH, ROPE, ELECTRIC CABLES, CHARGER, TRACKING DEVICE. I'M ALL SET.

HANG ON, DR. CROSS. I'M NOT GOING TO LET YOU GO ALONE. I'M COMING WITH YOU.

THANKS, TONY, YOU'RE A GOOD FRIEND. COME ON THEN--LET'S GO BEFORE WE CHANGE OUR MINDS.

WHEN WE GET BACK, THE INDESTRUCTIBLE MAN SHOULD HAVE FINISHED CHARGING.

THE FURNISS ESTATE.

ARE YOU SURE THIS IS THE BEST WAY IN?

WELL, IT KEEPS US OUT OF THE WAY OF THOSE SECURITY CAMERAS.

LET'S JUMP FOR IT.

WOOOAHHHH!

TONY? WHERE ARE YOU?

I APPEAR TO BE IN A SHRUB. BUT THERE'S NO LASTING DAMAGE.

ARE YOU STILL PICKING UP THE SIGNAL?

YUP, AND IT'S GETTING STRONGER. IT'S COMING FROM THE BACK OF THE BUILDING.

IT'S NUMBER THREE!

SO THE RUMOURS WERE TRUE. ANOTHER ONE DID SURVIVE THE COLOSSUS.

OKAY, WE'VE GOT TO GET HIM OUT OF HERE BEFORE FURNISS TAKES HIM APART LIKE THOSE OTHER ROBOTS. LOOK, THAT SIGNAL LIGHT IS FLASHING, SO SOME SYSTEMS MUST STILL BE WORKING.

LET'S POWER HIM UP. THEN WE CAN MOVE HIM.

IT'S A GOOD THING WE BROUGHT THESE CABLES.

NOW, LET'S SEE...

WE'LL HAVE TO GIVE HIM A SHORT EMERGENCY CHARGE. I THINK I REMEMBER HOW TO ACCESS HIS SHORT CHARGE POWER POINTS.

THERE'S SOME DAMAGE HERE THAT LOOKS RECENT. SOMEONE'S BEEN TRYING TO OPEN HIM UP.

CONNECTING TO THE CHARGE PACK NOW.

RIGHT, LET'S SEE IF THIS WORKS. FINGERS CROSSED...

SPUT!

SPUT!

PLIIING!

HE'S COMING ROUND!

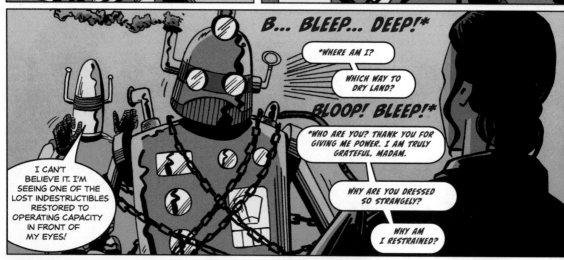

B... BLEEP... DEEP!*

*WHERE AM I?

WHICH WAY TO DRY LAND?

BLOOP! BLEEP!*

*WHO ARE YOU? THANK YOU FOR GIVING ME POWER. I AM TRULY GRATEFUL, MADAM.

WHY ARE YOU DRESSED SO STRANGELY?

WHY AM I RESTRAINED?

I CAN'T BELIEVE IT. I'M SEEING ONE OF THE LOST INDESTRUCTIBLES RESTORED TO OPERATING CAPACITY IN FRONT OF MY EYES!

I'VE NO IDEA WHAT YOU'RE SAYING, BUT DON'T WORRY. WE'RE GOING TO GET YOU OUT OF HERE.

WHAT'S ALL THIS RACKET?

UH-OH!

THE METAL MAN. IT'S WORKING!

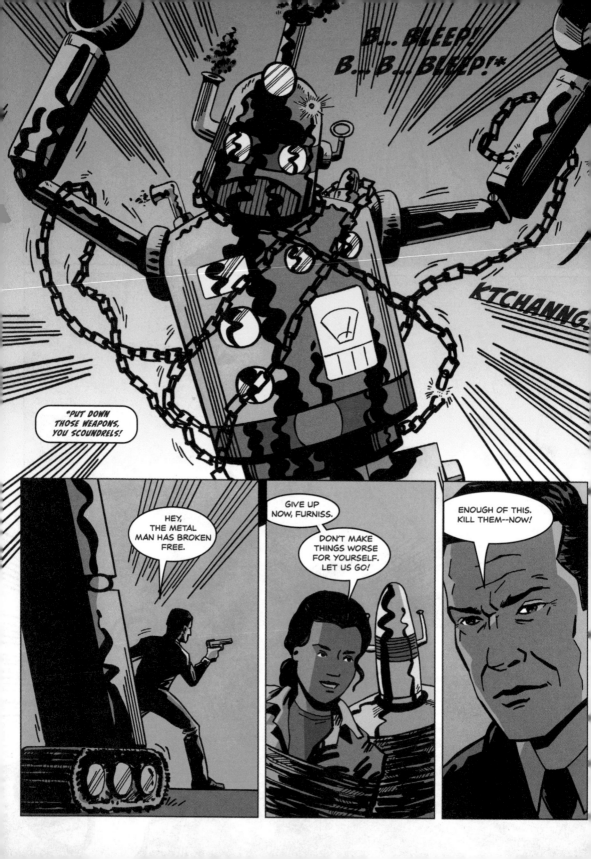

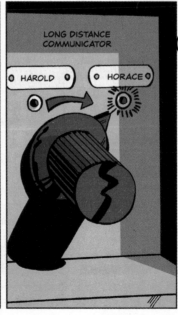

FINISH

6

START

1

14 APRIL 1912: THE *COLOSSUS* SINKS. METAL MAN NUMBER TWO, ALSO KNOWN AS HAROLD, BEGINS HIS EPIC VOYAGE ACROSS THE SEABED.

6 APRIL 1972: METAL MAN NUMBER TWO EMERGES FROM THE SEA ONTO THE ROBOT CITY DOCKS AND SHUTS DOWN ALMOST IMMEDIATELY.

ROUTE OF THE COLOSSUS

METAL MAN NUMBER TWO'S INCREDIBLE SEA JOURNEY

2

JULY–OCTOBER, 1923: HAROLD REMAINS STATIONARY FOR SEVERAL MONTHS-- REASON UNKNOWN.

5

MAY 1958: HAROLD ENCOUNTERS A GIANT SQUID.

4

OCTOBER 1946: STRONG CURRENTS CAUSE PROBLEMS.

3

DECEMBER 1930: THE MID- ATLANTIC RIDGE PROVES NEARLY INSURMOUNTABLE.